THIS WALKER BOOK BELONGS TO:

_____

_____

_____

_____

For Andrew

First published 1999 by Walker Books Ltd
87 Vauxhall Walk, London SE11 5HJ

2 4 6 8 10 9 7 5 3 1

© 1999 Vanessa Cabban

This book has been typeset in Horley Old Style.

Printed in Hong Kong

British Library Cataloguing in Publication Data
A catalogue record for this book is
available from the British Library.

ISBN 0-7445-6155-8 (hb)
ISBN 0-7445-6786-6 (pb)

Bertie and Small
and the Brave Sea Journey

Vanessa Cabban

WALKER BOOKS
AND SUBSIDIARIES
LONDON • BOSTON • SYDNEY

Bertie and Small

play together every day.

Small is the rabbit and Bertie
wears the hat with long floppy ears.

Bertie and Small make a house

but it's not big enough
and it's too hot.

"Ooof!" says Bertie.

Bertie takes Small for a car ride.
Vroom! Vroom! Vroom!

Bertie hides inside the
box with Small.

"Let's sail across the sea," says Bertie.
"Watch out for sea-snakes."

A storm comes and
the boat shivers and shakes.

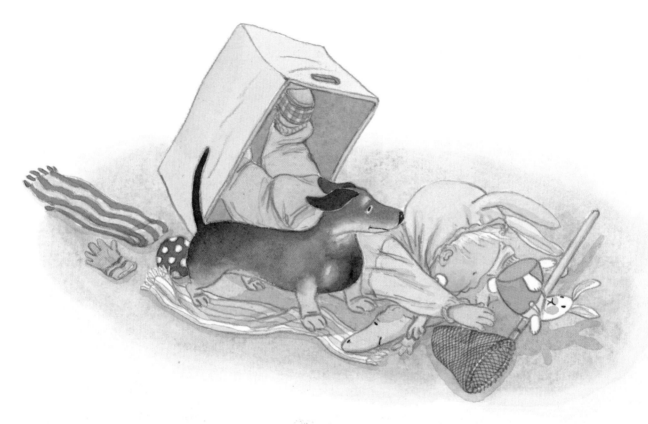

Small falls overboard and Bertie

tumbles out behind him.

"Youch!" says Bertie.

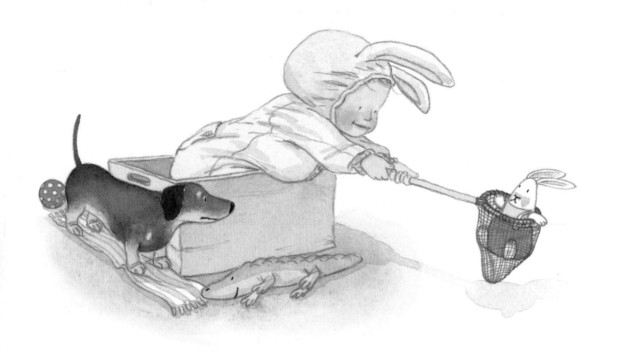

But Bertie is clever and Small is brave
and they save each other.

And then Daddy comes.

"Play with us, Daddy," says Bertie.

Daddy is the ship's engineer and
Bertie and Small are the navigators.

They say Boo! to the crocodile
and Huh! to the sea-snakes.

Then Bertie and Small
and Daddy go ashore for a drink.

"The storm was rough," says Bertie.
"Small was really brave."

MORE WALKER PAPERBACKS
For You to Enjoy

BERTIE AND SMALL'S FAST BIKE RIDE
by Vanessa Cabban

Another delightful book about Bertie and his soft-toy rabbit.
In this story they're going on a fast bike ride – around the world!

0-7445-6785-8   £3.99

MY FRIEND HARRY
by Kim Lewis

James takes his toy elephant Harry everywhere –
around the farm, on holiday, to bed…
Then, one day, James starts school.

"An altogether charming picture book…
Bound to be a much-returned-to-favourite with 3 – 6 year olds."
The Junior Bookshelf

0-7445-5295-8   £4.99

Walker Paperbacks are available from most booksellers, or by post from B.B.C.S., P.O. Box 941, Hull, North Humberside HU1 3YQ

24 hour telephone credit card line 01482 224626

To order, send: Title, author, ISBN number and price for each book ordered, your full name and address,
cheque or postal order payable to BBCS for the total amount and allow the following for postage and packing:
UK and BFPO: £1.00 for the first book, and 50p for each additional book to a maximum of £3.50.
Overseas and Eire: £2.00 for the first book, £1.00 for the second and 50p for each additional book.

Prices and availability are subject to change without notice.